Watch It Grow

Mealworms

by Martha E. H. Rustad
Consulting editor: Gail Saunders-Smith, PhD

Consultant: Laura Jesse
Plant and Insect Diagnostic Clinic
Iowa State University, Ames, Iowa

Mankato, Minnesota

Pebble Books are published by Capstone Press,
151 Good Counsel Drive, P.O. Box 669, Mankato, Minnesota 56002.
www.capstonepress.com

e 595.769
RUS

1 2 3 4 5 6 14 13 12 11 10 09

Library of Congress Cataloging-in-Publication Data
Rustad, Martha E. H. (Martha Elizabeth Hillman), 1975–
    Mealworms / by Martha E.H. Rustad.
    p. cm. — (Pebble books. Watch it grow)
    Includes bibliographical references and index.
    Summary: "Simple text and photographs present the life cycle of mealworms"
— Provided by publisher.
        ISBN-13: 978-1-4296-2226-4 (hardcover)   ISBN-10: 1-4296-2226-1 (hardcover)
        ISBN-13: 978-1-4296-3443-4 (softcover)   ISBN-10: 1-4296-3443-X (softcover)
    1. Meal worms — Life cycles — Juvenile literature. I. Title.
QL596.T2R87 2009
595.76'9 — dc22   2008026934

Note to Parents and Teachers

The Watch It Grow set supports national science standards related
to life science. This book describes and illustrates mealworms.
The images support early readers in understanding the text. The
repetition of words and phrases helps early readers learn new
words. This book also introduces early readers to subject-specific
vocabulary words, which are defined in the Glossary section. Early
readers may need assistance to read some words and to use the
Table of Contents, Glossary, Read More, Internet Sites, and Index
sections of the book.

Table of Contents

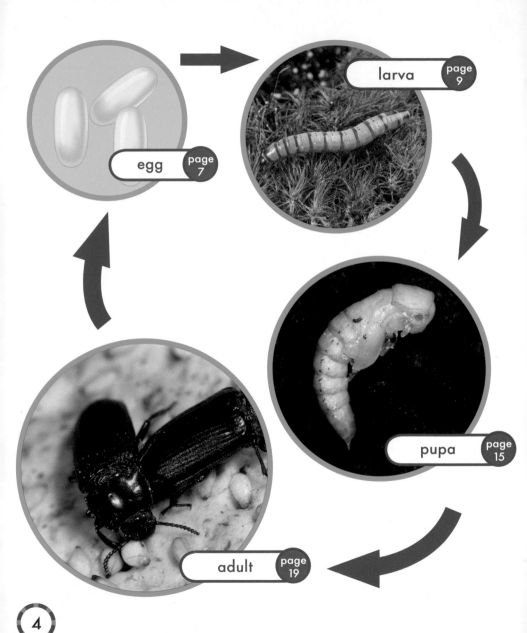

egg **page 7**

larva **page 9**

pupa **page 15**

adult **page 19**

Metamorphosis

Mealworms are insects.
They are young
darkling beetles.
Darkling beetles go through
metamorphosis as they grow.

eggs

From Egg to Larva

Darkling beetles
begin life as tiny eggs.
A female lays eggs
in grain, in the ground,
or on rotting plants.

larva

After about two weeks,
mealworms hatch
from the eggs.
Mealworms are
also called larvae.

10

Mealworms dig underground.
They eat insects
and dead leaves.
Some mealworms eat
corn or wheat.

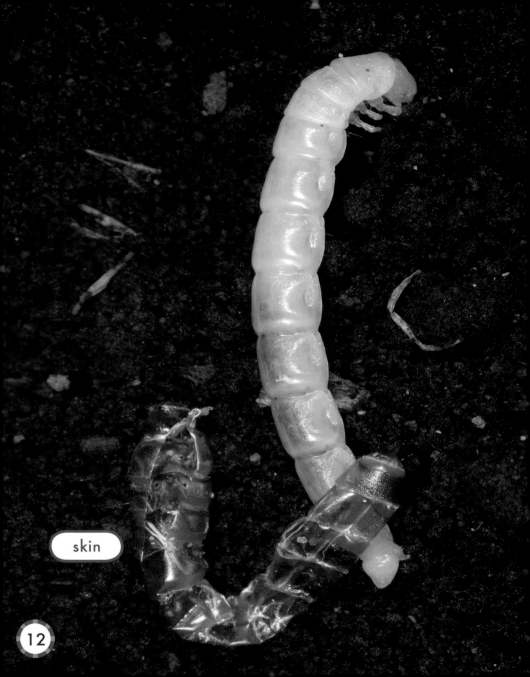

skin

Mealworms molt many times as they grow.
Their old skin falls off.
Mealworms grow quickly before the new skin hardens.

pupa

From Pupa to Adult

Mealworms molt and grow
for one to three months.
After the last molt,
mealworms become pupae.

Pupae stay underground.
They do not move.
The pupae are growing
adult wings and six legs.

Pupae crack open
in one to four weeks.
Adult beetles come out.
At first, they have
soft, white bodies.

Adults harden
and turn black after a day.
Males and females mate.
Females lay eggs.
The life cycle begins again.

Glossary

grain — the seed of a cereal plant such as wheat, rice, corn, rye, or barley

hatch — to break out of an egg

insect — a small animal with a hard outer shell, six legs, three body sections, and two antennae; most insects have wings.

larva — an insect at the stage between egg and pupa; the plural of larva is larvae.

metamorphosis — the series of changes some animals go through as they develop from eggs to adults

molt — to shed an outer shell or layer of skin so a new covering can be seen; when this process happens once, it is also called a molt.

pupa — an insect at the stage between a larva and an adult; the plural of pupa is pupae.

Read More

Hartley, Karen, Chris Macro and Philip Taylor. *Beetle.* Bug Books. Chicago: Heinemann Library, 2008.

Salas, Laura Purdie. *From Mealworm to Beetle: Following the Life Cycle.* Amazing Science: Life Cycle. Minneapolis: Picture Window Books, 2009.

Internet Sites

FactHound offers a safe, fun way to find educator-approved Internet sites related to this book.

Here's what you do:

1. Visit *www.facthound.com*

2. Choose your grade level.

3. Begin your search.

This book's ID number is 9781429622264.

FactHound will fetch the best sites for you!

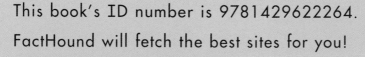

Index

Word Count: 136
Grade: 1
Early-Intervention Level: 17

Editorial Credits
Erika L. Shores, editor; Alison Thiele, designer; Marcie Spence, photo researcher

Photo Credits
Alamy/Nikki Edmunds, 18
Capstone Press/Alison Thiele, 4 (eggs), 6 (eggs); Karon Dubke, cover (larva), 1, 4 (larva), 8
Dwight R. Kuhn, cover (adult and pupa), 4 (pupa and adult), 10, 12, 14, 16, 20
Visuals Unlimited/Science VU, 6